Study Guide

Identifying the Seed

An Examination and Evaluation of the Differences
between Dispensationalism and Covenant Theology

Robert McKenzie

ISBN:
ISBN-13: 978-1-7239-2797-3

CONTENTS

INTRODUCTION

This study guide is designed to help the reader navigate through each chapter of the book, *Identifying the Seed*. It is my hope that the study questions will be a good resource for the reader. Included at the end of each lesson is a personal application question to encourage the reader to go beyond the specific teachings of the book. It can also be used by the reader to engage with the discussion by writing down personal thoughts or questions that arise during the reading. This study guide is designed to be used by either individuals or by groups.

There is a book recommendation at the end of each lesson for further study. Some of the books are denser than others, but all are excellent examples of books that can help the reader dig into each subject deeper. At the end of *Identifying the Seed*, I included an extensive bibliography, but in the study guide I am suggesting an essential reading list. Be assured, there are many other good books out there on these subjects that you may prefer. Neither in the book nor in the study guide did I include the list of the thousands of sermons that I listened to during my research. Instead, I have included a template for listening to any sermon.[1] I believe this will be a helpful article to read. It is my hope that both the book and the study guide will increase the knowledge of the subjects and promote better communication amongst brethren. Above all, my goal is to bring glory to our God.

---

[1] I am including a link to Dr. Phil Ryken's excellent article on how to listen to sermons.
http://www.reformation21.org/articles/how-to-listen-to-a-sermon.php

1

INTRODUCTION TO BOOK
AND REFORMED HERMENEUTICS

The purpose of this book is to foster a better understanding between Dispensationalists and Reformed believers. We are brothers and sisters in Christ and should seek to love and understand one another. A major misunderstanding that I discuss in the book is how Dispensationalists surmise the way Reformed believers interpret Scripture. This misunderstanding is probably the greatest obstacle to beneficial dialogue. The two sides are closer than they think in how they approach the way the Bible is to be interpreted, so this should not hinder our continued dialogue. In fact, it should encourage it.

How would you answer someone who says that we shouldn't worry about theology until we get to Heaven?

Why is it important to study these issues?

Which should come first: theology or the Bible? Why?

What misconception does Dispensationalism often have regarding the Reformed hermeneutic?

What are the true differences in the hermeneutics between Dispensationalism and Reformed Theology?

What do Dispensationalists often say when they describe the hermeneutics of Reformed Theology?

What does R. C. Sproul teach regarding Reformed hermeneutics? What does *sensus literalis* mean, and what does it not mean?

What does it mean that the Bible interprets itself? Why is this important to our study?

What is progressive revelation?

What does the passage concerning the road to Emmaus have to do with our study?

What is the main area of doctrine that is at the heart of our discussion?

Application question: Am I charitable in allowing other Christians to explain what they believe and why they believe it, or do I only hear what I already think they believe?

Book recommendation: *Knowing Scripture* by R. C. Sproul

2

THE COVENANT OF REDEMPTION

The Covenant of Redemption is a theological term that is often used in Covenant Theology. Like any theological term, it is only there to describe something about God. Never be afraid of terms—even the word *Christian* is a term. Everyone needs to take the time to understand what a term means and how it is being used. This will take time, but it is the best way to learn. In this case, the term is being used to help us understand the functions of each member of the Trinity in the salvation of the elect.

Why might the term *Covenant of Redemption* be something a Dispensationalist has never heard of?

How does Reformed Theology understand the term *Calvinism*?

What is a good way to understand the structure of theology?

Do the majority of Dispensationalists teach multiple ways of salvation?

Why is the Covenant of Redemption important?

How does this covenant help us understand God?

What Scriptures are used to support the Covenant of Redemption?

What is a doctrinal statement or a confession?

What does Covenant Theology consider the first purpose of man towards God?

Application Question: How does a Christian worship all the members of the Trinity?

Book recommendation: *The Christ of the Covenants* by O. Palmer Robertson

3

THE COVENANT OF WORKS

If you spend any time watching TV, movies, or reading the latest novel, it will not take you long to notice that in general anyone who is not a Christian has the same basic world view. It goes something like this: "All people are essentially good. If there is a god, he or she is not concerned with our little lives. If there is a heaven, most people go there. If there is a hell, only really bad people go there. I am one of the good people."

Scripture tells us a different story. All people are actually in a very real and binding relationship with God. All people are considered sinners and are under the very judgment of God. Unless God's wrath is appeased, all will suffer judgment for their sins. Because Adam represented us in the garden and broke the Covenant of Works, we are all covenant breakers and guilty of this sin. We have died spiritually, and unless our spiritual nature is regenerated to life there is no hope. The only hope is if our debt could be paid.

How do both Covenant Theology and Dispensationalism use theological terms that are not found in Scripture? Is this a good or bad way to study theology?

How does O. Palmer Robertson define a covenant?

What does the Covenant of Works teach?

Was Adam created neutral—neither good or bad? How does this affect the teaching of the Covenant of Works?

What was the result of Adam breaking the Covenant of Works?

What does it mean that Adam acted as the Covenant Head of the entire human race?

How does this relate to Christ?

What is Original sin?
  The Reformed understanding:

  The Arminian understanding:

What is the age of accountability?

What examples does Scripture give of regeneration from the womb?

What does Genesis 3:15 teach about salvation? Why is this so important?

Application Question: How does understanding the doctrine of original sin help me in my evangelism?

Book Recommendation: *No Adam, No Gospel: The History of Redemption* by Richard Gaffin

4

THE COVENANT OF GRACE

Due to Adam's failure in the garden, all people walk this world as covenant breakers—not as righteous or neutral but as sinners. God promised to send a Savior who would provide the way for our forgiveness. God's decision to save anyone is purely out of grace and mercy.

We deserve wrath, and since God cannot overlook sin there must be atonement. In order to redeem us, Jesus takes our punishment upon Himself so that we might be spared. God's choice of election is not arbitrary. He makes His choice of salvation not from among people who are righteous or neutral but from among the justly condemned. This choice therefore is both undeserved and gracious. Our salvation is secure because God will not break His gracious covenant.

What is the Covenant of Grace?

Some will say that the doctrine of election makes God arbitrary. Is that true? Why or why not?

How does the doctrine of total depravity relate to God's sovereign choice in election?

What are some of the Scriptures that teach the doctrine of election?

What was the mission of Christ?
    According to Covenant Theology:

    According to Dispensationalism:

Does Dispensationalism teach that Jesus always intended to go to the cross?

Why does Covenant Theology see a contradiction in the Dispensational interpretation of the mission of Christ?

How does Jesus accomplish our salvation?

According to Reformed Theology, what is taught in John 6:37-40?

What can we learn about Jesus' mission and His Kingdom in Jesus' conversation with Pilot?

What does the Noahic Covenant teach?

Application Question: How does the mission of Christ apply to me personally?

Book Recommendation: *Christ and Covenant Theology: Essays on Election, Republication, and the Covenants* by Cornelis Venema

5a

THE ABRAHAMIC COVENANT

The Abrahamic Covenant is a major key to understanding the Bible. God promised in Genesis 3:15 that the Seed of the woman would crush the head of the seed of the serpent. This is the introduction of the Covenant of Grace. The Abrahamic Covenant is the continuation of that Covenant. There are some key promises made in this covenant that are helpful in understanding the disagreements between the two systems of theology. Are these promises fulfilled in Christ at the time of His first advent, or are they fulfilled in Israel in the Millennial Kingdom? The answer to this question is at the heart of our discussion.

What were God's promises in the Abrahamic Covenant?

What do Dispensationalists misunderstand concerning what Covenant Theology is teaching regarding the Abrahamic Covenant? Why is this a problem?

What is the main disagreement between Dispensationalism and Covenant Theology in regards to the Abrahamic Covenant?

What do the passages in Joshua have to do with the fulfillment of the land promise?

Why were the Israelites able to lose the blessings that they had been given under the Mosaic Covenant?

What is the Dispensational response given by Michael J. Vlach?

How does Hebrews 4 interpret the giving of the land under Joshua?

Application question: What often happens when we try to fix our problems in ways that God has not commanded?

Book Recommendation: *The Abrahamic Covenant in the Gospels* by Theophilus Herter

5b

THE ABRAHAMIC COVENANT FULFILLED

The law of God is very important. Paul tells us in the first chapter of Romans that God's law is demonstrated for the Jewish people in the Law of Moses. The thing is, the Gentiles didn't have the Law of Moses, so how can they be held responsible for breaking God's law? Paul goes on to say in the same chapter that God's law is inherently written on our hearts. So although Gentiles were never under the Law of Moses, they still had the law of God, and are therefore responsible for their disobedience.

Israel was the visible representative of the people of God leading up to the time of Christ. They were given the land of Canaan and were to be witnesses to the surrounding nations. But Israel and the blessings that they received were typological to the ultimate realities of the true fulfillment of the Abrahamic Covenant in Christ. Jesus is the second Adam, and He is the true Israel who does not give in to temptation, who fulfills the law completely, and who receives the blessings of the Abrahamic Covenant. He is the Seed of the woman who crushed the head of the seed of the serpent.

How does a double fulfillment help us understand the promises made in the Abrahamic Covenant?

What does Paul tell the Galatians concerning the purpose of the Law?

Who fulfills the promises made in the Abrahamic Covenant?
According to Covenant Theology:

According to Dispensationalism:

What leads Dispensationalists' to think that Covenant Theology teaches that the Church replaces Israel?

What does Reformed Theology actually teach?

How does Romans 9 help us understand how the Abrahamic Covenant is fulfilled?

According to Paul, who are the true children of Abraham?

What does John the Baptist teach us about the true children of Abraham?

What does Jesus teach us about the true children of Abraham?

Who does Covenant Theology conclude are the true children of Abraham?

Application question: What is the importance to my life that I am considered a child of Abraham?

Book Recommendation: *Prophecy and the Church* by Oswald T. Allis

6

THE MOSAIC COVENANT
(AND DAVIDIC AND PALESTINIAN)

The Abrahamic Covenant flows through the Mosaic Covenant. The typological fulfillment of the promises made to Abraham are seen embodied in the nation of Israel. However, these blessings were lost due to the disobedience of the people. Instead, they received the curses. Even at the time of exile, the people were given hope. There would be a new covenant that would someday come to replace the old Mosaic Covenant. This new covenant would include a descendent of David who would rule as king for eternity in an eternal land.

What is the key to understanding the Mosaic Covenant?

How is the Mosaic Covenant part of the Covenant of Grace?

What was the nation of Israel's relationship to the Mosaic Covenant?

What happened to the nation of Israel because of the people's disobedience?

What does Dispensationalism teach happened in 1948?

Why must the nation of Israel have the temple in order to function as the nation of Israel?

What did Jesus come to do in His first advent?
    According to Covenant Theology:

    According to Dispensationalism:

What does the Davidic Covenant teach, and what is the key passage?
    For Dispensationalism:

    For Covenant Theology:

What is the Palestinian Covenant?

What passages does Dispensationalism use for the Palestinian Covenant?

How would Covenant Theology understand these passages?

What is the difference between the teachings of Ryrie and the teachings of Vlach regarding these passages?

Application Question: If God always keeps His promises, what does that mean for my life?

Book Recommendation: *Putting Amazing Back into Grace* by Michael Horton

7

THE NEW COVENANT

Whenever the Lord's Supper is celebrated in church, we are reminded that through Christ we have entered into a new covenant. No longer is the law of God written on stone tablets, now the law of God is written on our hearts. The New Covenant and the Kingdom of God function together. In the New Covenant, we are brought from the Covenant of Works into the Covenant of Grace. Peter at Pentecost declared that the New Covenant that had been spoken of by the prophets had come, and Paul tells us the same thing in Romans. The book of Hebrews points to these prophecies being fulfilled in Christ for eternity.

What does God promise the people of Israel in Jeremiah 31?

What happens to the Old Covenant when the New Covenant comes?

Is the New Covenant already here, or is it still in the future? How do we know?

According to Covenant Theology, how is the Abrahamic Covenant fulfilled?

What does the Lord's Supper teach us concerning the New Covenant?

Why did Jesus send the Holy Spirit?

Using Joel, what is Peter telling us happens at Pentecost in Acts 2?

What do Hebrews 8 and Jeremiah 31 teach us about the New Covenant?

What happened to the temple in 70 AD? What did that mean for the nation of Israel?

How does the finished work of Jesus relate to the temple?

Application Question: How does Jesus being the fulfillment of the Abrahamic/New Covenant help me personally?

Book Recommendation: *Saved by Grace* by Anthony A. Hoekema

8a

THE TWO-AGE MODEL

The language in the New Testament that talks about *this age* and *the age to come* is an indication that we are experiencing the fulfillment of the Abrahamic Covenant but not the complete fulfillment. The Kingdom of God has broken into this world, and the very gates of Hell will not stand against it. Now, we experience living with sin, pain, sorrow, etc. The wisdom of this age is foolishness; people war against God and each other. Someday, we will live in a world where there is no sin or pain, where there are no longer any wars or rumors of wars. We will be eternal, and we will all be family with no strife of any kind. For now, we will live in this age, waiting for the age to come.

What are the two worlds that Christians live in?

Do people who are not Christians know God and if they do, what are the results?

Why shouldn't it surprise us that Christians are persecuted?

How are the people of God supposed to live during this age?

What are the signs of this age as described in Matthew 24?

How can we sum up this present age?

How does Scripture contrast this age and the age to come?

In what sense has the age to come already begun for the Christian?

What happens on The Last Day?

Application Question: What does Scripture teach concerning my relationship with other Christians, and how should that affect my life?

Book recommendation: *The Covenant of Grace* by Geerhardus Vos

8b

THE PARABLES

The parables are an excellent way for us to understand what happens at the end of the age when Christ returns. The Gospel goes out to the whole world and there are some who believe and some who reject its message. This time of proclamation is now, when the ruler of this world is actively trying to stop and to destroy the children of God. The Kingdom will grow from a small stone to an enormous mountain from a small seed to a large tree. At the end of this age, Christ will return, and at that time believers will be separated from unbelievers. This is the wheat being separated from the chaff or the good fish from the bad fish. Unbelievers will be cast into judgment for eternity, and believers will go on into their eternal reward.

Why should Christians care about the physical world?

Are the Kingdom of God and the Kingdom of Heaven talking about two different kingdoms? Why or why not?

What does the parable of the sower teach us about the Kingdom during this age?

What do the parables of Matthew 13 teach us about the Kingdom?

What do the parables that use money teach us about the Kingdom?

What do the parables using everyday life teach us about the Kingdom?

What event transports us from this age into the age to come?

Application Question: What do the parables teach me about what I should be concerned about in this life?

Book recommendation: *The Parables* by Simon Kistemaker

9

THE SECOND COMING

One of the greatest divisions between Dispensationalism and Covenant Theology is what happens at the Second Coming. For Dispensationalists, first there is a Rapture where the Church will be removed from the Earth. Then, a seven year tribulation period will commence before the Second Coming takes place. Covenant Theology teaches that the people of God who are alive at the time of Christ's return will be raptured or caught up to Him as He is returning to the Earth. There will then be a final judgment, and God will create the New Heavens and the New Earth. When Christ returns, there will be loud shouts, trumpet blasts, and all those who oppose Him will be defeated. When Christ returns, all of His enemies will have been made a footstool for His feet—including death itself.

What or who is judged at the Second Coming?

What made the believers in the church in Thessalonica fearful?

What does Paul tell them will happen at the Second Coming?

What is the significance of death being judged at the Second Coming? Why might this be a problem for the Dispensational system?

What doctrine has become the most associated with Dispensationalism, and what Scripture do they use?

What events occur at the Second Coming?

Application question: How does the fact that Christ can return at any moment affect your daily life? Should it?

Book recommendation: *The Coming of the Kingdom* by Herman Ridderbos

10a

THE HISTORY OF DISPENSATIONALISM AND COVENANT THEOLOGY

The history of theology does not determine what we believe; the Bible does. What we must remember, however, is that the history of theology is the record that we have of fellow believers and even non-believers struggling with and developing what they believe the Bible is teaching. Covenant Theology can trace many of its doctrines back to the Early Church Fathers for commonality regarding what the Bible is teaching. For a long time, Dispensationalists claimed that they could also look back and see their core distinctives taught throughout Church history. One of the main claims was that because many in the early church believed in premillennialism and Dispensationalism was premillennial, that Dispensationalism was taught by the early Church. However, there are some major differences between the premillennialism of the early Church and the premillennialism of Dispensationalism. Today, some Progressive Dispensationalists understand and teach that Dispensationalism was developed under John Nelson Darby recognizing that Church history supports a covenantal framework.

Why should we study historical theology?

What is our ultimate authority for our theology?

When was Dispensationalism first developed?

What does Dispensationalism teach concerning the early Church and premillennialism?

Was the early church premillennial?

According to Ryrie what was the main cause of how premillennialism was lost in the early Church?

What is Charles E. Hill's conclusion regarding the eschatological understanding of the Early Church Fathers?

What does Justin tell Trypho concerning the eschatology of the Early Church Fathers?

What does the story regarding the grandchildren of Jude teach us?

Why does the presence of premillennialism in the early Church not prove the historicity of Dispensationalism?

In what ways was Covenant Theology taught by the Early Church Fathers?

Application Question: What are some great benefits of studying the history of theology through Church history?

Book recommendation: *Regnum Caelorum: Patterns of Millennial Thought in Early Christianity* by Charles E. Hill

10b

THE FOUNDING OF DISPENSATIONALISM

John Nelson Darby is the founder of Dispensationalism and one of the founders of the Brethren Church movement. While recovering from an accident, Darby came to the conclusion that the Bible was sectioned into different epochs in which God worked differently. He taught that there were two peoples of God: Israel and the Church. Dispensationalism did not catch on in England, but it did in America through prophecy conferences and periodicals. C. I. Scofield took the teachings of Dispensationalism and used them to create a widely popular study Bible. Lewis Sperry Chaffer's systematic theology and the founding of Dallas Theological Seminary helped popularize the teaching that became widespread in America in the middle and second half of the twentieth century.

Why did Darby become disillusioned with the Anglican Church?

What did Darby help to start?

Who was James Brooks? Why was he significant in early Dispensationalism?

Who was C. I. Scofield? What were his contributions to early Dispensationalism?

Why is the interpretation of II Timothy 3:16 so important to the relationship between the Reformed and Dispensationalism?

Who was Lewis Sperry Chafer? What were his contributions to Dispensationalism?

What has been the Dispensationalist's attitude toward creeds and confessions?

Who was Charles C. Ryrie? How did Dispensationalism change in the 1950s?

Application Question: How should Christians who disagree handle their disagreements?

Book Recommendation: *Backgrounds to Dispensationalism: Its Historical Genesis and Ecclesiastical Implications* by Clarence Bass

11

THE HERMENEUTICS OF DISPENSATIONALISM

One thing that needs to be understood about Dispensationalists is that they have a high regard for the Bible. They correctly teach that the Bible is true, that it is the ultimate authority for the Christian, and that above all it must be interpreted literally. When they say that the Bible must be interpreted literally, they mean that to interpret in any other way would stray from truth itself. If anyone seeks to interpret the Bible in any other way, their interpretation is instantly called into question as false. The Reformed also believe that we should interpret the Bible literally; only we also understand that there are allegories and metaphors that are in Scripture that are also intended to tell us what is true. The key to understanding the Bible is allowing the Bible to interpret itself. Dispensationalism believes the Bible needs to be interpreted according to its divisions and according to the understanding that God has two peoples with two distinct programs. Unless you interpret the Bible with these presuppositions, they believe that you will be interpreting the Bible as if you were wearing a blindfold.

What does Dispensationalism believe in regards to how they practice hermeneutics and how everyone else practices hermeneutics?

According to Ramm and Pentecost's conclusion, unless you are interpreting Scripture according to the Dispensational method of interpretation, what will the result be?

What reason does Pentecost give as to why the Reformed interpret
Scripture in the way they do?

What is the key to discussing misconceptions and misunderstandings
between the two sides?

What does Pentecost teach in regards to the interpretation of prophesy?

How does Lindsey use his book *The Late Great Planet Earth* to interpret
the book of Revelation?

What may have led to Dispensationalism's decline in the late 1980s?

What keeps Dispensationalism united as Dispensationalism?

How does C. I. Scofield define a dispensation?

What three elements does a dispensation need to have in order for it to be a dispensation?

1.

2.

3.

How does Dispensationalism define Israel and the Church?

Israel:

The Church:

How does Covenant Theology define Israel and the Church?

Israel:

The Church:

Application Question: What does the unity of the people of God mean for how I interact with fellow Christians?

Book recommendation: *Dispensationalism: Rightly Dividing the People of God?* by Keith Mathison

12

THE SEVEN DISPENSATIONS:
DISPENSATIONS 1 – 5

A dispensation has three parts: a people, a promise or test, and (if it is broken) a punishment. The first five dispensations divide history into ways that can be easily understood. If all Dispensationalism was doing was looking at different time periods of history, there would not be as much difference between the two systems. However; Dispensationalism is teaching that in each of these periods of time the people who are under that dispensation have the ability to obey God and pass the test of that dispensation. This chapter lists the Dispensational pattern of history up until Pentecost in Acts 2.

What is the first dispensation called? What does it teach?

How was the first dispensation broken? What was the result?

What is the second dispensation called? What does it teach?

How was the second dispensation broken? What was the result?

What is the third dispensation called? What does it teach?

How was the third dispensation broken? What was the result?

What is the fourth dispensation called? What does it teach?

Why is it hard for Covenant Theologians to understand how Dispensationalism can teach both a dispensation and also a covenant made with Abraham?

How does Dispensationalism try to solve this problem?

What three promises are given in the fourth dispensation?
1.

2.

3.

How was the fourth dispensation broken? What is the result?

For Dispensationalism, with whom was the Abrahamic Covenant made?

What is the fifth dispensation called? What does it teach?

How was the fifth dispensation broken?

Application Question: What does the Abrahamic Covenant mean for me personally?

Book recommendation: *Dispensationalism Today* by Charles Ryrie

12b

THE SEVEN DISPENSATIONS:
DISPENSATIONS 6 – 7

The final two dispensations truly show the divide between the two systems. Did Christ come to offer a renewed and restored political nation to the people of Israel, or did Jesus come bringing a kingdom with Him? Is this Kingdom present and active, or is it future? The Dispensational belief in the rejection of Christ by the people and the subsequent creation of the Church as Plan B is one of the greatest puzzlements to the Reformed. The Dispensation of the Kingdom is filled with so many fascinating details that most Covenant Theologians shake their head in confusion. For Dispensationalism, the details are extensive but understandable. Though it frustrates them that other people don't see these details in Scripture, they remain undeterred in their interpretation.

How does Dispensationalism interpret the anticipation of the Jewish people at the time of Christ's first advent?

How does Covenant Theology interpret the anticipation of the Jewish people at the time of Christ's first advent?

According to Dispensationalism, how is the offer of the Kingdom at the time of Christ to be understood?

According to Dispensationalism, what did the rejection of the Kingdom lead to?

According to Dispensationalism, what was unknown even after Pentecost?

What does Dispensationalism point to when trying to prove the Church came into existence only after Pentecost?

What is the sixth dispensation called? What does it teach?

How would the sixth dispensation be broken? What is the result?

What is the seventh dispensation called? What does it teach?

What is something that will shock Covenant Theologians in regards to the dispensational teaching of the seventh dispensation?

How would the seventh dispensation be broken? What is the result?

Application Question: What does the finished work of Christ mean for my everyday life?

Book recommendation: *Understanding Dispensationalists* by Vern Poythress

13a

THE TRIBULATION PERIOD: PART 1

The tribulation period serves a dual purpose for Dispensationalism; the world will be judged for their rejection of Christ and the failure of the dispensation, and the Jews will be brought to repentance. The Jewish people will once again be made into a nation and will repent. Those who survive the Great Tribulation will come into the Kingdom in natural physical bodies and will repopulate the Earth. For Dispensationalism, the establishment of the current state of Israel was the sign that the times of the Gentiles would soon be over and that God would once again start the prophetic clock for His people Israel.

What often holds the most attention for Dispensationalists in their theology?

How can understanding literary genre help with the study of the Bible?

Why is the seven-year tribulation period necessary for Dispensationalism?

What happened in 1948 that Dispensationalism points to as evidence for its system?

For Dispensationalism, what does Daniel 9 have to do with the Tribulation?

What is the objection to the Dispensational interpretation of Daniel 9 offered by Covenant Theology?

What problem does Covenant Theology have when interpreting Daniel chapter 9?

How do both sides interpret the Antichrist or Man of Sin?

Dispensationalism:

Covenant Theology:

How do world events influence or affect many Dispensationalists?

How is the time of Jacob's trouble from Jeremiah 30 interpreted by Dispensationalism?

According to Dispensationalism, who are the 144,000 found in Revelation 7 and 14?

According to Dispensationalism, who are the two witnesses from Revelation 11?

Application question: How do I understand the tribulations of this world?

Book recommendation: *The Man of Sin* by Kim Riddlebarger

13b

THE TRIBULATION PERIOD: PART 2

The details of the tribulation period are hard to keep straight even for Dispensationalists. Their interpretation is so different than what you would find in Covenant Theology that they often leave someone who is Reformed just shaking his head. Dispensationalists are not trying to be fantastical or compete with H. G. Wells. They are trying to be faithful to Scripture knowing that they are interpreting the very Word of God, and so every word is important. The dispensation of the tribulation period will end with the Second Coming. The Church was removed seven years earlier at the Rapture, but now Christ is coming to set up His Kingdom and to take His place on the throne of David. He will reign as Lord and King over Israel for 1,000 years.

What happens to the Church during the time of the seven year tribulation?

How does Dispensationalism interpret the four horsemen of the apocalypse?

How does Dispensationalism interpret what happens when the seven seals are opened?
1st

2nd

3rd

4th

5th

6th

7th

How does Dispensationalism interpret what happens when the seven
trumpets are blown?

1st

2nd

3rd

4th

5th

6th

7th

How does Dispensationalism understand the number 666 or the Mark of
the Beast?

How does Dispensationalism interpret what happens in the seven bowl
judgments?

1st

2nd

3rd

4th

5th

6th

7th

For Dispensationalism, what happens in the battle of Armageddon?

For Dispensationalism, what happens at the Second Coming of Christ?

Application Question: How does the news each day affect me? How
should it?

Book recommendation: *The Bible and the Future* by Anthony Hoekema

14a

THE MILLENNIAL KINGDOM

Although the Millennial Kingdom will be set up with Christ ruling from the throne of David and Israel as the nation that rules the world, for Dispensationalism, there will be some believing Gentiles who survive the tribulation period. These Gentiles will go into the world living in the Kingdom, and through them the nations of the world will once again be established. They will be ruled by Christ from His throne in Israel, they will have to come to the Temple to make sacrifices, and they will eventually fill the Earth. Satan will be bound at this time until the 1,000 years end. Satan will go out into these nations and turn them from Christ leading to the final rebellion that is quickly destroyed by Christ. At the end of the Kingdom, God will make a New Heavens and a New Earth so that both the Church and Israel will forever be with the Lord.

For Dispensationalism, what will be fulfilled in the Millennial Kingdom?

For Dispensationalism, where will the Church be during this time?

How does Craig A. Blaising describe the Kingdom?

What kinds of sacrifices has Dispensationalism historically taught will be given at the temple in the Millennial Kingdom?

How does Covenant Theology challenge this teaching?

What does Progressive Dispensationalism teach regarding a new temple and sacrifices in the Millennial Kingdom?

What problems do the Progressives face by using this interpretation?

How does the present reality of the New Covenant in the Church present a problem for Dispensationalism?

How does Ryrie try to fix this problem?

According to Dispensationalism, what happens to the Church and Israel for the rest of eternity?

Application question: What does the unity of believers mean for my relationships at Church?

Book recommendation: *The Millennial Kingdom* by John Walvoord

14b

THE MILLENNIAL TEMPLE

One of the greatest changes in Dispensationalism over the last thirty or so years has been the integration of some of the benefits of the New Covenant; Progressive Dispensationalism realized that to have a temple in the Millennial Kingdom complete with sacrifices was to ignore the teaching of the book of Hebrews. For Dispensationalists who are not progressive, the rejection of a new temple in the Millennial Kingdom was to ignore the teaching of the book of Ezekiel. The binding of Satan and the peace of the Kingdom are subjects of major disagreement between the two sides. Covenant Theology believes that the binding of Satan began at the time of Christ and is accomplished through the Gospel. Dispensationalism teaches that if that were true then why is there sin and evil in the world? Dispensationalism points to Revelation 20 as proof that the Kingdom is still future as well as proof that the Reformed are in error by spiritualizing the text.

What do the Reformed reference in regards to why the Levitical Law has been done away with?

What priesthood is Jesus a part of through the cross?

How does the book of Hebrews link this priesthood with the New Covenant?

What does Hebrews 10 tell us about the Old Covenant?

When does Dispensationalism believe the fulfillment of the New Covenant will be?

What must be present in the nation of Israel in order for it to function as the nation of Israel?

Why do literal sacrifices in the Millennial Kingdom create problems for the Dispensational system?

Does Ezekiel speak of sin offerings or of memorial offerings?

How does Covenant Theology interpret these passages in Ezekiel?

What does Hebrews 8-10 teach concerning the Old Covenant sacrifices?

What does Dispensationalism teach concerning the binding of Satan in Revelation 20?

What does Covenant Theology teach concerning the binding of Satan in Revelation 20?

What does Dispensationalism teach will happen at the end of the Millennial Kingdom?

What happens at the final judgment at the end of the Millennial Kingdom?

Application Question: If the Gospel binds Satan, then how should that affect my confidence in the Gospel?

Book recommendation: *Things to Come: A Study in Biblical Eschatology* by J. Dwight Pentecost

BOOK LIST

I've given you twenty book recommendations. In case you want to start with less than 20, here is the list of the books from "must reads" to "advanced."

MUST READ:

Michael Horton. *Putting Amazing Back into Grace*

O. Palmer Robertson. *The Christ of the Covenants*

R. C. Sproul. *Knowing Scripture*

Theophilus Herter. *The Abrahamic Covenant in the Gospels*

Simon Kistemaker. *The Parables*

Richard Gaffin. *No Adam, No Gospel: The History of Redemption*

FOR FURTHER STUDY:

Oswald T. Allis. *Prophecy and the Church*

Clarence Bass. *Backgrounds to Dispensationalism: Its Historical Genesis and Ecclesiastical Implications*

Anthony Hoekema. *The Bible and the Future*

Keith Mathison. *Dispensationalism: Rightly Dividing the People of God?*

Vern Poythress. *Understanding Dispensationalists*

Kim Riddlebarger. *The Man of Sin*

Charles Ryrie. *Dispensationalism Today*

J. Dwight Pentecost. *Things to Come: A Study in Biblical Eschatology*

John Walvoord. *The Millennial Kingdom*

ADVANCED STUDY:

Charles E. Hill. *Regnum Caelorum: Patterns of Millennial Thought in Early Christianity*

Anthony A. Hoekema. *Saved by Grace*

Herman Ridderbos. *The Coming of the Kingdom*

Cornelis Venema. *Christ and Covenant Theology: Essays on Election, Republication, and the Covenants*

Geerhardus Vos. *The Covenant of Grace*

Milton Keynes UK
Ingram Content Group UK Ltd.
UKHW011306120124
435922UK00001B/133